What Is the Lord's Supper?

Crucial Questions booklets provide a quick introduction to definitive Christian truths. This expanding collection includes titles such as:

Who Is Jesus?

Can I Trust the Bible?

Does Prayer Change Things?

Can I Know God's Will?

How Should I Live in This World?

What Does It Mean to Be Born Again?

Can I Be Sure I'm Saved?

What Is Faith?

What Can I Do with My Guilt?

What Is the Trinity?

TO BROWSE THE REST OF THE SERIES,
PLEASE VISIT: **REFORMATIONTRUST.COM/CQ**

CQ

What Is the Lord's Supper?

R.C. SPROUL

IR *Reformation Trust* A DIVISION OF LIGONIER MINISTRIES, ORLANDO, FL

What Is the Lord's Supper?
© 2013 by R.C. Sproul

Published by Reformation Trust Publishing
a division of Ligonier Ministries
421 Ligonier Court, Sanford, FL 32771
Ligonier.org   ReformationTrust.com

Printed in China
RR Donnelley
0001018
First edition, sixth edition

ISBN 978-1-64289-051-8 (Paperback)
ISBN 978-1-64289-079-2 (ePub)
ISBN 978-1-64289-107-2 (Kindle)

Cover design: Ligonier Creative
Interior typeset: Katherine Lloyd, The DESK

All Scripture quotations are from the ESV® Bible (The Holy Bible, English Standard Version®), copyright © 2001 by Crossway, a publishing ministry of Good News Publishers. Used by permission. All rights reserved.

Library of Congress Cataloging-in-Publication Data

Sproul, R.C. (Robert Charles), 1939-2017
  What Is the Lord's Supper? / R.C. Sproul.
    pages cm. -- (The crucial questions series ; no. 16)
  ISBN 978-1-56769-328-7
1. Lord's Supper. 2. Evangelicalism. 3. Reformed Church--Doctrines. I.
Title.
  BV825.3.S67 2013
  234'.163--dc23
                            2013013850

Contents

One   The Significance of the Passover........1

Two   The Institution of the Lord's Supper 13

Three The Consummation of the Kingdom 21

Four   Real Body and Blood? 31

Five   The Natures of Christ...............41

Six   The Presence of Christ.............47

Seven Blessing and Judgment 55

Chapter One

The Significance
of the Passover

At the very heart of the life and worship of the early Christian community was the celebration of the Lord's Supper. In the early days of church history, the celebration of Holy Communion was known by different names. On the one hand, the early church used to come together and celebrate what they called an "agape feast" or a "love feast" in which they celebrated the love of God and the love that they enjoyed with one another as Christians in this holy supper. The sacrament was called the Lord's Supper because it made reference to the last supper that Jesus had with His disciples in the Upper Room on the night before His death. In the early church and later, the Lord's Supper was called the "Eucharist," taking its definition from the Greek verb *eucharisto*, which is the Greek verb that means "to thank." Thus, one facet of the Lord's Supper has been the gathering of the people of God to express their gratitude for what Christ accomplished in their behalf in His death.

The Lord's Supper is a drama that has its roots not only in that Upper Room experience, but the roots reach back into the Old Testament celebration of Passover. In fact, you will recall that before Jesus instituted the Lord's Supper in the Upper Room, He had given requirements to His disciples that they would secure a room for the purpose of their meeting together on this occasion because He was entering into His passion. He knew that His trial, death, resurrection, and return to the Father were imminent, so He said to His disciples, "I deeply desire to celebrate the Passover with you one last time."

The immediate context in which Jesus instituted the Lord's Supper was the celebration of the Passover feast with His disciples. The link to Passover is seen not only in His words to the disciples but also in similar language used by the Apostle Paul when he wrote to the Corinthian church. He wrote, "Christ, our Passover lamb, has been sacrificed" (1 Cor. 5:7). It's clear that the Apostolic community saw a link between the death of Christ and the Old Testament Passover celebration.

For us to get a handle on that, we have to look back to the pages of the Old Testament to the historical context of the institution of the Passover. We must remember the enslavement of the people of Israel in Egypt under the domination of a ruthless pharaoh. Recall that the people suffered greatly, and they moaned and they groaned in their suffering, but their groaning did not go unheard. We understand that God appeared in the Midianite wilderness to the aged Moses who was living in exile as a fugitive from the forces of Pharaoh at that time. When God appeared to Moses and spoke to him out of the burning bush, He said, "Do not come near; take your sandals off your feet, for the place on which you are standing is holy ground" (Ex. 3:5).

In that encounter, God directed Moses to go both to Pharaoh and to the Jewish people to deliver the Word of God to them. We recall that Moses felt inadequate for the task and wondered how he was going to be able to communicate the Word of God with any authority to either

Pharaoh or the people of Israel. Essentially, Moses said, "Why would they follow me? Why should they believe me?" And to paraphrase it, God replied: "Look, you go. You tell them I've heard the cry of My people, and you tell Pharaoh that I say, 'Let My people go that they can come and worship me on the mountain where I will show them,' and you tell the people to pack up and to leave Pharaoh and Egypt." So God empowered Moses with the ability to perform miracles in order to authenticate the origin of this incredible message.

From there, what took place was a contest of will and power between God, through Moses, and the magicians of Pharaoh's court. In a very short time the tricks of the magicians were exhausted, and the power of God was made manifest through Moses in dramatic ways. There were ten plagues in all, but it's in the first nine that we see an escalation of drama and conflict between Moses and Pharaoh. One plague would befall the Egyptians. Then, Pharaoh would relent and say, "Okay, leave; take your people and go." But as soon as the phrase left the lips of Pharaoh, God would step in and harden Pharaoh's heart. This was to make it very clear to the people of Israel that their redemption was from the hand of God and not from the grace of

Pharaoh. So, another contest would ensue. Another plague would befall the Egyptians, Pharaoh would relent, God would harden Pharaoh's heart and he would keep the people in captivity. Then another contest would ensue, then another, and then another, until finally, Pharaoh had just about all he could take from Moses, and he said: "Get away from me! Take care never to see my face again or you shall die." And Moses responded by saying, "You have spoken well, for I will never see your face again."

It was at this point in the drama where God announced to Moses the tenth plague that He would bring upon the Egyptians. This plague was the worst of all of the plagues because it involved the destruction of the firstborn sons of all of the Egyptians, including the firstborn son of Pharaoh. So God told Moses:

"Yet one plague more I will bring upon Pharaoh and upon Egypt. Afterward he will let you go from here. When he lets you go, he will drive you away completely. Speak now in the hearing of the people, that they ask, every man of his neighbor and every woman of her neighbor, for silver and gold jewelry." And the LORD gave the people favor in the sight of the Egyptians. Moreover, the man Moses was very great in the land of Egypt, in the sight of Pharaoh's servants and in the sight of the people. So Moses said, "Thus says the LORD: 'About midnight I will go out in the midst of Egypt, and every firstborn in the land of Egypt shall die, from the firstborn of Pharaoh who sits on his throne, even to the firstborn of the slave girl who is behind the handmill, and all the firstborn of the cattle. There shall be a great cry throughout all the land of Egypt, such as there has never been, nor ever will be again. But not a dog shall growl against any of the people of Israel, either man or beast, that you may know that the LORD makes a distinction between Egypt and Israel.' And all these your servants shall come down to me and bow down to me, saying, 'Get out, you and all the people who follow you.' And after that I will go out." And he went out from Pharaoh in hot anger. Then the LORD said to Moses, "Pharaoh will not listen to you, that my wonders may be multiplied in the land of Egypt." (Ex. 11:1–9)

Then, in the beginning of the twelfth chapter of Exodus, God brought Moses to Himself and instituted the celebration of the Passover. We must consider the following narrative from the book of Exodus because it has such a dramatic impact on the future life of the Jewish nation. This is the institution that is celebrated in the Upper Room between Jesus and His disciples:

The LORD said to Moses and Aaron in the land of Egypt, "This month shall be for you the beginning of months. It shall be the first month of the year for you. Tell all the congregation of Israel that on the tenth day of this month every man shall take a lamb according to their fathers' houses, a lamb for a household. And if the household is too small for a lamb, then he and his nearest neighbor shall take according to the number of persons; according to what each can eat you shall make your count for the lamb. Your lamb shall be without blemish, a male a year old. You may take it from the sheep or from the goats, and you shall keep it until the fourteenth day of this month, when the whole assembly of the congregation of Israel shall kill their lambs at twilight. Then they shall take some of the blood and put it on the two doorposts and the lintel of the houses in which they eat it. They shall eat the flesh that night, roasted on the fire; with unleavened bread and bitter herbs they shall eat it. Do not eat any of it raw or boiled in water, but roasted, its head with its legs and its inner parts. And you shall let none of it remain until the morning; anything that remains until the morning you shall burn. In this manner you shall eat it: with your belt fastened, your sandals on your feet, and your staff in your hand. And you shall eat it in haste. It is the LORD's Passover. For I will pass through the land of Egypt that night, and I will strike all the firstborn in the land of Egypt, both man and beast; and on all the gods of Egypt I will execute judgments: I am the LORD. The blood shall be a sign for you, on the houses where you are. And when I see the blood, I will pass over you, and no plague will befall you to destroy you, when I strike the land of Egypt." (Ex. 12:1-13)

This is critical because we know that the sacraments of the New Testament are understood in the life of the church both as signs and seals of something extremely important. A sacrament gives a dramatic sign that points beyond itself to some truth of redemption that is crucial to the life of the people of God. When God instituted the Passover in the Old Testament, He was saying to Moses, to paraphrase it:

Take this animal, the lamb that is without blemish, and kill it. Take its blood, and mark the entrance to your houses. Put the blood on the lintel of the door, on the doorpost, as a sign that marks you as the people of God, so that when the angel of death comes to smite the firstborn of the land, and to execute My judgment on the Egyptians, the destruction of that judgment will befall only the Egyptians. I'm going to differentiate between the people that I have called out of the world to be My covenant and holy people and those who have enslaved them. So My wrath will fall on Egypt but not on My people. The angel will pass over every home that is marked by the blood of the lamb.

The sign character of this ritual was really a sign of deliverance. It was a sign of redemption because it meant that these people would escape the wrath of God.

Ultimate calamity is exposure to the wrath of God. Christ saves His people from the wrath of the Father. Not only are we saved *by* God, but we are saved *from* God, and that idea is dramatically displayed in the Passover as recorded in the book of Exodus. The sign on the doorpost, the sign marked by the blood of the lamb meant that the Israelites would be rescued from calamitous exposure to the wrath of God.

So that night, the angel of death came and killed the firstborn of the Egyptians, but the people of God were spared. After that, Moses led them out of bondage, through the Red Sea, into the Promised Land, where they became God's people under the covenant of Moses, receiving the law at Mount Sinai. They did go out and worship God at His sacred mountain, but as a perpetual remembrance of this redemption, every year thereafter, the people of Israel obeyed the institution of the Passover. They gathered in their homes, and they ate the food and bitter herbs, and they drank the wine, all of which they did to remember the salvation God had wrought for them in the land of Egypt. They participated in this original celebration with their staffs in their hands, as people who were ready to move, ready to march at any second because the Lord said they were to be ready to move out of Egypt, out of bondage into the Promise Land as soon as Pharaoh and his forces were destroyed.

When Jesus celebrated His final Passover with His disciples, He departed from the standard liturgy in the middle of the celebration. He added a new meaning to the Passover celebration as He took the unleavened bread, attaching a new significance to it when He said, "This is My body which is broken for you." Then, after the supper had been completed, He took the wine and he said, in effect, "I'm attaching a new significance to this element as you celebrate the Passover because this wine is my blood. Not the blood of the lamb in the Old Testament whose blood was marked on the doorpost, but now this cup is my blood." In essence, Jesus was saying, "I am the Passover; I am the Pascal Lamb; I am the one who will be sacrificed for you. It is by My blood being marked over the door of your life that you will escape the wrath of God." So He said: "From now on, this is My blood, which is shed for you for the remission of your sins. This is the blood of a new covenant." This new covenant that He instituted that very night fulfills the old covenant, giving it its fullest and most meaningful expression.

Chapter Two

The Institution of the Lord's Supper

In Luke 22 we read:

Then came the day of Unleavened Bread, on which the Passover lamb had to be sacrificed. So Jesus sent Peter and John, saying, "Go and prepare the Passover for us, that we may eat it." They said to him, "Where will you have us prepare it?" He said to them, "Behold, when you have entered the city, a man carrying a jar of water will meet you. Follow him into the house that he enters and tell the master of the house, 'The Teacher says to you, Where is the guest room, where I may eat the Passover with my disciples?' And he will show you a large upper room furnished; prepare it there." And they went and found it just as he had told them, and they prepared the Passover.

And when the hour came, he reclined at table, and the apostles with him. And he said to them, "I have earnestly desired to eat this Passover with you before I suffer. For I tell you I will not eat it until it is fulfilled in the kingdom of God." And he took a cup, and when he had given thanks he said, "Take this, and divide it among yourselves. For I tell you that from now on I will not drink of the fruit of the vine until the kingdom of God comes." And he took bread, and when he had given thanks, he broke it and gave it to them, saying, "This is my body, which is given for you. Do this in remembrance of me." And likewise the cup after they had eaten, saying, "This cup that is poured out for you is the new covenant in my blood. But behold, the hand of him who betrays me is with me on the table. For the

Son of Man goes as it has been determined, but woe to that man by whom he is betrayed!" (vv. 7–22)

In this description of the institution of the Lord's Supper, we see that Jesus refers specifically to two dimensions of time—the present and the future. In our culture, we generally measure the passing of time by referring to the past, the present, and the future. When we look at the meaning and significance of the Lord's Supper in the life of the Christian community, we see that it has significance and application to all three dimensions of time.

The Lord's Supper is related to the past by virtue of its link to the Passover. In addition, what Jesus talked about in the Upper Room has since taken place, so His death on the cross is past to us as well. He tells the disciples that they were to do this sacrament "in remembrance of Him." To the extent that our celebration of the Lord's Supper is a remembrance, the focus is on what took place in the past.

Oftentimes, in the Bible, we see what we call the sacralization of space and of time. That is, we see countless examples where God or His people Israel, gave sacred, holy, and consecrated significance to particular times and to particular events that took place in their world. Consider

Moses' call by God in the Midianite wilderness: "Then he said, 'Do not come near; take your sandals off your feet, for the place on which you are standing is holy ground'" (Ex. 3:5). What God was saying to Moses was, "Moses, this place on the planet is now sacred; this is a holy site." What made the ground holy was not the fact that Moses was there. It was holy ground because it was a point of intersection between God and His people. If you go through the Old Testament, you will see special places where God met with His people or acted mightily on behalf of His people. In these instances, it was often customary for the people to mark the spot. Usually it was done by building a very simple altar with stones.

For example, when Noah landed on the top of Mt. Ararat and exited from the ark, one of the very first things he did was build an altar there to remember the place where God had delivered him and his family from the deluge. After the children of Israel passed over the Jordan under the leadership of Joshua, they erected a monument. We see this again and again. When Jacob had his midnight vision of God ascending and descending from the heavens as he was on his way to find a wife, he named that spot Bethel because he said, "Surely the LORD is in this place, and I did not know it" (Gen. 28:16). So he took the stone that he had used for a pillow during the night and he anointed it with oil and placed it there as a marker since God had appeared to him in the dream and had made His promise to him.

In the Bible, time and again, we see the sacralization of space. We do it today as well. A few years ago, there was a tragic and fatal traffic accident very close to my home in which one of the victims was a little girl who was a gymnast. She lived across the street from me, and on my way to work every day, I pass the tree where the car crashed. To this day, there are all kinds of memorials, flowers, and crosses marking the spot where she died. We all have special places in our lives. They may be special for good or bad reasons, but we count these places as holy to us, sometimes with physical markers

Not only do we have sacred space in Scripture, but we also have sacred time. The festivals of the Old Testament involved the sacralization of time. With respect to the Passover, God ordained for the people of Israel to celebrate annually their redemption from slavery in Egypt by marking a sacred moment on the calendar for the feast of the Passover. This was sacred time.

We mark sacred days on the church calendar as well.

We go to church on Sundays to remember the fact that Jesus was raised on Sunday morning. We celebrate the feast of Pentecost. We celebrate Easter and Christmas. We celebrate these things because, as human beings, it is strongly rooted in our humanity to have sacred time. We want to remember those moments that are most important to us in history. We celebrate our own birthdays as if there were something sacred about them. They are sacred in the sense that they're extraordinary and special to us. It's good to remember the day in which we came into this world. We celebrate wedding anniversaries because we want to remember the significance of them.

I'm sure our Lord understood this human need to recapitulate and recollect important moments. When He gathered with His disciples in the Upper Room, one of the elements of this institution was His command to repeat this supper in remembrance. "Do this in remembrance of me" (Luke 22:19). In a sense, what Christ said is that "I know that I've been your teacher for three years. I've done many things, some of which you're going to forget; but whatever else, please don't forget this because what you are going to experience in the next twenty-four hours is the most important thing that I will ever do for you. Don't ever forget it. You are remembering me. You are remembering My death, the pouring out of My blood, the breaking of My body, which will occur on the morrow. Please don't ever forget it." And so, for two thousand years, the church has remembered the death of Christ in this sacred memorial of the Lord's Supper.

Jesus also understood the traditional Jewish link between apostasy and forgetting. Linguistically, that link is found in the very word *apostate*, which means "a letting go of or forgetting." An apostate is somebody who has forgotten what he once was committed to. We remember Psalm 103, where David cries, "Bless the Lord, O my soul! And *forget not* all of his benefits."

Jesus died two thousand years ago, and not one second passes on the clock that there aren't people somewhere in this world sitting down, breaking bread, drinking wine, and remembering Christ's death until He comes.

Chapter Three

The Consummation
of the Kingdom

In Luke's gospel we read, "You are those who have stayed with me in my trials, and I assign to you, as my Father assigned to me, a kingdom, that you may eat and drink at my table in my kingdom and sit on thrones judging the twelve tribes of Israel" (22:28–30).

Here Jesus focused on the future orientation of the consummation of His kingdom. He is the Anointed One whom the Father has declared to be the King of kings and Lord of lords. He mentioned that His Father has bestowed upon Him a kingdom, and in like manner He now bestows upon His disciples the kingdom of God and promises that there will be a time in the future when He will sit with them at His table. Implied in this statement from Jesus is the anticipated promise of the marriage feast of the Lamb, the great ceremony of Christ and His bride, which will take place in heaven (Rev. 19:6–10).

First, let's look to the Old Testament, where we see some brief hints of this future expectation. Psalm 23 reads as follows:

> The LORD is my shepherd; I shall not want. He makes me lie down in green pastures. He leads me beside still waters. He restores my soul. He leads me in paths of righteousness for his name's sake. Even though I walk through the valley of the shadow of death, I will fear no evil, for you are with me; your rod and your staff, they comfort me. (vv. 1–4)

David likened the Lord God to a shepherd. David himself came from the ranks of the shepherds, so he knew the imagery of which he was speaking. He knew it is the task of the shepherd to tend the sheep. If you've ever seen a flock of sheep, you know how they're aimless in their meanderings unless somebody is leading them. In this text, the Good Shepherd takes the sheep into the green pastures, places them not by the rapids where they might fall into the water and die, but gives them a place near tranquil pools of water. These are safe places to drink and satisfy their thirst. Then the Shepherd leads the sheep in the paths of righteousness. Even though they walk through the valley of the shadow of death, they aren't afraid, because the Shepherd is with them. He comforts them by His staff and His rod. He uses the rod to defend the sheep from wolves, and He uses the staff to herd them and keep them in His safe presence.

In the midst of all of these beautiful images of God as a good shepherd, David goes on to say, "You prepare a table before me in the presence of my enemies; you anoint my head with oil; my cup overflows" (v. 5). God vindicates His people, and He vindicates them in the presence of those who have falsely accused them. In essence, David said, "Not only does He prepare a table before me, but He prepares this table and invites me to His table publicly." Not only do they enjoy a feast at His table, but the cup that is set before them flows over with the wine that makes the heart glad. In a very real sense, this psalm anticipates the Messiah, who comes as the Good Shepherd. This Messiah is also the same one who refers to Himself as the living bread that has come down from heaven (John 6:51). From the Old Testament image of the shepherd, the New Testament shows the fulfillment in Christ Jesus, the Good Shepherd who lays down His life for His sheep, and who is not a hireling who flees when the wolves come. Yet at the same time, He also fulfills the historic experience of the provision of foodstuffs from heaven by way of the manna during the wilderness experience of the Jews. God gave them daily provisions to satisfy their physical needs by feeding them manna from heaven. That image is employed in the New Testament when Jesus is called the "Bread of heaven" who comes down from heaven to feed and nurture His people.

In order to understand that consummation of the Kingdom in the Lord's Supper, we must look at Matthew 22 and the parable of the Wedding Feast.

> And again Jesus spoke to them in parables, saying, "The kingdom of heaven may be compared to a king who gave a wedding feast for his son, and sent his servants to call those who were invited to the

wedding feast, but they would not come. Again he sent other servants, saying, 'Tell those who are invited, "See, I have prepared my dinner, my oxen and my fat calves have been slaughtered, and everything is ready. Come to the wedding feast."' But they paid no attention and went off, one to his farm, another to his business, while the rest seized his servants, treated them shamefully, and killed them. The king was angry, and he sent his troops and destroyed those murderers and burned their city. Then he said to his servants, 'The wedding feast is ready, but those invited were not worthy. Go therefore to the main roads and invite to the wedding feast as many as you find.' And those servants went out into the roads and gathered all whom they found, both bad and good. So the wedding hall was filled with guests. But when the king came in to look at the guests, he saw there a man who had no wedding garment. And he said to him, 'Friend, how did you get in here without a wedding garment?' And he was speechless. Then the king said to the attendants, 'Bind him hand and foot and cast him into the outer darkness. In that

place there will be weeping and gnashing of teeth.'
For many are called, but few are chosen." (vv. 1–14)

In this parable, there is a frightening element of judgment as well as an exciting promise of unspeakable blessing. Remember that when Christ came, His entrance into the world was defined in terms of the Greek word *krisis*, from which we get the English word *crisis*. His coming brought the supreme division—between those who would embrace Him and those who would reject Him. We are told in John 1:11 that Jesus came to His own, namely, to the Jewish nation, but His own people received Him not. In a sense, this parable is a recapitulation of the history of Israel, whom God invited to be His bride. But they refused to come to His wedding feast. They were not interested. They had better things to do. So they left and went home. They went and did everything but respond to the invitation to the wedding feast that their Lord God had offered. When the servants went out to invite them, they murdered the servants. Who were those people? Obviously, they were the prophets of Israel who were murdered by God's chosen people. Finally, God said, "My Son is going to have a bride, a kingdom, a wedding where there will be a multitude of guests." So He sent servants out into the highways and the byways to find people who were not part of the original community. This obviously refers to God's bringing in Gentiles who were strangers and foreigners to the covenant of Israel. He gives these people to the Son to celebrate the marriage with His bride.

In the book of Revelation, we have references to the marriage feast of the Lamb. In chapter 19, we read:

After this I heard what seemed to be the loud voice of a great multitude in heaven, crying out, "Hallelujah! Salvation and glory and power belong to our God, for his judgments are true and just; for he has judged the great prostitute who corrupted the earth with her immorality, and has avenged on her the blood of his servants." Once more they cried out, "Hallelujah! The smoke from her goes up forever and ever." And the twenty-four elders and the four living creatures fell down and worshiped God who was seated on the throne, saying, "Amen. Hallelujah!" And from the throne came a voice saying, "Praise our God, all you his servants, you who fear him, small and great." Then I heard what seemed to be the voice of a great multitude, like the roar of many waters and like the sound of mighty peals of thunder, crying out, "Hallelujah! For the Lord our God the Almighty reigns. Let us rejoice and exult and give him the glory, for the marriage of the Lamb has come, and his Bride has made herself ready; it was granted her to clothe herself with fine linen, bright and pure"—for the fine linen is the righteous deeds of the saints. And the angel said to me, "Write this: Blessed are those who are invited to the marriage supper of the Lamb." And he said to me, "These are the true words of God." Then I fell down at his feet to worship him, but he said to me, "You must not do that! I am a fellow servant with you and your brothers who hold to the testimony of Jesus. Worship God." For the testimony of Jesus is the spirit of prophecy. (vv. 1–10)

In this final book of the New Testament, we have the opportunity to see a glimpse into the future. Here John sees the marriage feast of the Lamb that is ready for His bride, the Church. There will come a day when all who are faithful to Christ will be gathered together in heaven for this joyous celebration, for this final marriage to Christ, which will be marked by a feast that would surpass anything that we could imagine in this world.

Knowing this future promise that runs throughout the teaching of the New Testament, we see references to it in the institution of the Lord's Supper. Jesus calls attention to the future time when He will sit down with His people and celebrate at the feast of the kingdom of God in heaven. There still remains a grand celebration. Every time we celebrate the Lord's Supper in this world, we shouldn't *only* look back to Christ's past accomplishments, but to the future feast that is yet to be fulfilled. There is still more of the kingdom of God for us to experience. We have experienced the inauguration of the kingdom in Christ's life, death, and resurrection, but we still await the final, future consummation of the kingdom. So when we celebrate the Lord's Supper, we see that it's not just a sign of what has already happened, but it's also a sign and seal of what will happen in the future.

In the Old Testament, God's people Israel celebrated the Passover once a year. This Passover looked forward to a future fulfillment, when the Pascal Lamb was sacrificed on Calvary. Today, every time we celebrate the Lord's Supper, we look into the future as well, to the promise of the wedding feast of Christ and His bride. In this way, the Lord's

Chapter Four

Real Body and Blood?

What is the present significance of the celebration of the Lord's Supper? We've seen its past and the future significance, but what about the present? It's at this point that the vast majority of the controversies surrounding the Lord's Supper have emerged.

Throughout church history, most people have favored the view that the real presence of Christ is present at the Lord's Supper. In other words, we are in a real communion with Him at the table. Of course, not everybody believes that there's any special way in which He's present at the Lord's Supper, but that's clearly the minority report. In any case, the controversy regarding the presence of the Christ in the Supper goes even deeper. The majority has agreed that Jesus is really present; the point of contention surrounds the mode of that presence. Christians have not agreed on the answer to this question: In what way is Christ present at the Lord's Table?

Part of the issue centers around how His presence is related to His words of institution. All three Synoptic Gospels report Jesus as saying, "This is my body." Historically, the question that has emerged in these controversies surrounds the word *is*. How must *is* be understood? When something is said "to be" something else, the verb *to be* serves as an equal sign. You can reverse the predicate and the subject without any loss in meaning. For example, if one says that "a bachelor is an unmarried man," there is nothing in the predicate that's not already present in the notion of bachelor in the subject. The term *is* in that sentence serves as an equal sign. We could reverse them and say, "An unmarried man is a bachelor."

In addition to this use of the verb *to be*, there is also the metaphorical use, where the verb *to be* may mean, "represents." For example, think of the "I am" statements of Jesus that are found in the Gospel of John. Jesus says, "I am the Vine, you are the branches. I am the Good Shepherd. I am the Door through which men must enter. I am the Way; I am the Truth; I am the Life." It's clear from any reading of those texts that Jesus is using the representative sense of the verb *to be* in a metaphorical way. When He says, "I am the Door," He is not crassly saying that where we have skin, He has some kind of wooden veneer and hinges. He means that, "I am," metaphorically, "the entrance point into the kingdom of God. When you enter a room, you have to go through the door. In the same way, if you want to enter God's kingdom, you've got to come through me."

When we arrive at the words of the institution of the Lord's Supper, the obvious question is, how is Christ using the word *is* here? Is Jesus saying, "This bread that I am breaking really is my flesh and this cup of wine that I've blessed is my blood?" When people are drinking the wine are they actually drinking His physical blood? When they are eating the bread, are they actually eating His physical flesh? That's what this controversy is about.

Remember, in first-century Rome, Christians were

accused of the crime of cannibalism. There were rumors that the Christians were meeting in secret places such as the catacombs to devour somebody's body and to drink that person's blood. Even that early in church history, the idea of a real connection between bread and flesh and the wine and blood had already appeared.

In the sixteenth century, the Lutherans and the Reformed found that the main barrier that kept them apart was their understanding of the Lord's Supper. They agreed on almost everything else. Martin Luther insisted on the identity meaning of the word *is* here. In the midst of the discussions, he repeated over and over the Latin phrase *hoc est corpus meum*—"this *is* my body." He insisted on this.

One of the major controversies of the sixteenth-century Reformation had to do with the Roman Catholic understanding of the Lord's Supper. The Roman Catholic Church's view then and now is what is known as transubstantiation. This is the view that the substance of the bread and wine are transformed supernaturally into the actual body and blood of Jesus when one participates in the Lord's Supper. But there was a simple objection to this view. When partaking of the Lord's Supper, the bread and wine still looked like, tasted, felt, smelled, and sounded like bread and wine. There was no discernible difference between the bread and wine before the consecration of the elements and after. A person could say, "You're telling me about a miracle of Christ really being physically present here, but it sure doesn't look like it. The elements seem exactly the same as they were beforehand."

In order to account for this problem, the Roman Catholic Church came up with a philosophical formula to account for the phenomenon of the appearances of bread and wine. They reached back into the past to the philosophical categories of Aristotle and borrowed his language to articulate their view.

Aristotle was concerned with the nature of reality and he made a distinction between the *substance* of an object and the *accidents* of an object. The term "accident" referred to an external, perceivable quality of a thing. If you were to describe me, you would describe me in terms of my weight, height, the clothes that I'm wearing, my hairstyle, the color of my face, or the color of my eyes. In all of these descriptions, you are restricted to my external, perceivable qualities. You don't know what I am in my personal essence. I don't know the true essence of a piece of chalk. I only see a cylindrical shape, hardness, and the color white. Those are all the outward perceivable qualities of chalk.

Aristotle believed that every object had its own substance and every substance had its corresponding accidents. If you had the substance of an elephant, you would also have the accidents of an elephant. For Aristotle, if it looked like a duck, walked like a duck, and quacked like a duck, it was a duck. The essence of duckness always produces the accidents of duckness. Any time you see the accidents of duckness, you know that what you can't see beneath the surface is the essence of duckness.

The medieval Western church borrowed from Aristotle's philosophical attempt to define the difference between surface perception and depth reality for the doctrine of transubstantiation. They said that in the Mass, a double miracle takes place. On the one hand, the substance of the bread and wine changes into the substance of the body and blood of Christ, while on the other hand, the accidents remain the same. What does that mean? Prior to the miracle, you have the substance of bread and the accidents of bread and you have the substance of wine and the accidents of wine. But after the miracle, you no longer have the substance of bread or the substance of wine. Instead, you have the substance of the body and blood of Christ, but you have the accidents of bread and wine remaining. Said differently, you have the accidents of bread and wine without their substances. The second miracle is seen in having the substance of the body and blood of Christ without the accidents of flesh and blood. That is the sense of the double miracle. You have the substance of one thing and the accidents of another. It is important to note that Aristotle himself would never have allowed for this line of thinking in the real world.

A few decades ago in Western Europe, there was a Dutch Roman Catholic theologian who published a work titled *Christ the Sacrament of the Encounter with God* in which he introduced a completely new idea. He said that what happens in the miracle of the Mass is not a supernatural transformation of the substance of one thing into the substance of another. It wasn't transubstantiation, but it was what he called *transignification*. He said that in the Mass, the elements of bread and wine take on a heavenly significance. There's a real change in the significance of the elements even though the nature of the elements remains the same. He was supported by the Dutch catechism and some other progressive theologians at that time, and it created a major controversy within the Roman Catholic Church. In 1965, the Pope published an encyclical titled *Mysterium Fidei*, "The Mystery of the Faith," in which he responded to this issue and said that not only is the content of the church's historic doctrine immutable, but its formulation is as well. He said the Aristotelian formulation of transubstantiation will continue to stand. That remains the official view of the Roman Catholic Church. This encyclical effectively rejected creative solutions offered by some to address the problem they perceived with transubstantiation.

Luther objected to transubstantiation because he believed it involved an unnecessary miracle. Luther believed that the real flesh and blood of Jesus were present in the elements, but they are in, with, and under them. The elements don't become the body and blood of Christ, but rather the body and blood of Christ are supernaturally added to the elements. In this sense, he still argued for the real presence of the physical body and blood of Christ.

The Reformed, such as John Calvin and many others, rejected Luther's view, though not on sacramental grounds but on Christological grounds. We'll seek to understand this rejection in the next chapter as we unpack the dual nature of Christ.

Chapter Five

The Natures of Christ

In order to understand Calvin's rejection of Luther's view of the Lord's Supper, we have to dig into church history for some help. Throughout the course of church history various heresies have been put forth concerning the human and divine nature of Christ.

In 451, at the Council of Chalcedon, the Church Fathers had to deal with these heresies on two different fronts. On the one hand, there was the Monophysite heresy, which was proposed by a man named Eutyches. According to

Eutyches, Christ had a nature that was neither fully divine nor fully human; rather, He had a single nature. One way to summarize his view would be to say that Christ had a deified human nature or a humanized divine nature. At the same time, at the other extreme, there was a heretic by the name of Nestorius. He argued that if you have two natures, then you must have two persons. He separated the divine and human natures.

At the Council of Chalcedon, the church declared that Christ is *vera homo, vera deus*. This means that Christ has two distinct natures—one that is truly human and one that is truly divine—that are united without confusion in a singular person. In this ruling, the church effectively addressed the heresy of Eutyches and Nestorius. Additionally, the church crafted what are commonly referred to as "The Four Negatives of Chalcedon." These "four negatives" are likely the most important formulation that came from this historic church council. At this fifth-century council, church leaders understood that what they were dealing with in the incarnation was a supreme mystery. They knew that they could not collectively say, in effect, "We have penetrated totally to the mystery of the incarnation." But they also wanted to affirm, without qualification, that there is a perfect union between the divine nature and the human nature, and that these two natures are genuine. But how, in fact, the unity of the incarnation is accomplished is still something that is shrouded in mystery. They also wanted to affirm that they understood enough to confidently reject current heresies that were threatening an orthodox understanding of the dual nature of Christ. The four negatives are as follows: the two natures are united without *mixture*, without *confusion*, without *separation*, and without *division*. However you understand the relationship between the human nature and the divine nature, you do not want to think of them in terms of being mixed together or confused. In His one person, Christ's humanity and deity can neither be swallowed up by the other nor can they be separated or divided.

Throughout church history, there have been persistent attempts to take one of Christ's two natures and use it to swallow the other. In liberal theology, the tendency has always been to end up with a Jesus who is purely human. This results in a Jesus who is not divine. The humanity swallows up the deity. On the other hand, at times we have also seen Christians who are overly zealous to protect the deity of Christ. In their zeal to protect biblical truth, they get so emphatic in reference to His deity that they unintentionally leave behind His humanity.

When we come to the New Testament, we see His humanity very clearly. He gets hungry, He gets thirsty, He weeps, and He bleeds. All of these elements manifest the true human nature that He possesses. God does not get hungry; God does not get thirsty; the divine nature doesn't bleed. Those are all aspects of the human nature. The answer to the question "to which nature does the body of Jesus belong?" is rather obvious. His physical body is a manifestation of His human nature, not His divine nature.

In addition to the four negatives, the Chalcedon confession ends with these words: "Each nature retains its own attributes." This means that in the incarnation, the divine nature does not stop being divine. It's right here that we approach the controversy surrounding the presence of Christ at the Lord's Supper. If each nature retains its own attributes, then what does it mean that the human nature retains its own attributes? Omnipresence is not an attribute of human nature. How is it possible for the human nature of Jesus to be at more than one place at the same time?

The Lutherans answered that objection by developing a novel understanding of the *communicatio idiomatum*—the "communication of attributes"—in reference to their doctrine of ubiquity. *Ubiquity* means "present here, there, and everywhere at the same time." It's a synonym for omnipresence. The Lutherans argue that if the divine nature has the ability to be present at more than one place at the same time, then that power and attribute of the divine nature is communicated to the human nature in the Supper. This made it possible for the human nature, including the human body of Christ, to be present everywhere at the same time. The human nature was endowed with a divine attribute. In contrast, the Reformed churches said that this violates Chalcedon by confusing the natures of Christ so that each nature does not retain its own attributes. This is why Calvin and others categorically rejected the Lutheran view of the Lord's Supper. Luther insisted on the corporeal presence of Jesus at more than one place at the same time. Our core beliefs concerning the nature of Christ are at stake in this, which is why the Reformed have affirmed the real presence of Jesus in the sacrament, but not in the same manner as Lutherans and Roman Catholics.

Chapter Six

The Presence
of Christ

In the Westminster Confession of Faith 29.7 we read
these words,

Worthy receivers, outwardly partaking of the
visible elements in this sacrament, do then also
inwardly by faith, really and indeed, yet not carnally and corporally, but spiritually, receive and
feed upon Christ crucified, and all benefits of His
death: the body and blood of Christ being then

not corporally or carnally in, with, or under the bread and wine; yet as really, but spiritually, present to the faith of believers in that ordinance, as the elements themselves are in their outward senses.

In our confession we see a distinction between the real presence of Jesus and the physical presence of Jesus. When it articulates this notion of the real presence of Jesus, what it means is that *spiritually speaking*, He is really present. What does that mean? First, let's consider what it doesn't mean. Sometimes we say, "I can't be with you next Sunday, but I'll be with you in spirit." What do we mean when we say that? It means that even though I'll be absent from you in terms of my physical location, I'll be thinking about you. You can count that as a type of spiritual presence. But we would hardly understand that sense of being present somewhere in spirit as being a real presence. This is certainly not what the confession means or what Reformers such as John Calvin meant when they talked about the real, spiritual presence of Christ in the Lord's Supper.

What did Calvin mean? First of all, let's begin with Calvin's important formula, which is expressed in the Latin phrase *finitum non capax infinitum*. This is a philosophical principle drawn from reason or logic. He was saying that the finite cannot contain the infinite. If you had an infinite amount of water, you could not contain that water in a six-ounce glass. Simple to understand, right?

With respect to the human nature of Jesus, Calvin said that the human body of Jesus could not contain the infinite deity of the Son of God. This is simply another way of saying that while the human body of Jesus is not omnipresent, the divine nature of Christ is. Yet Calvin not only said that Christ is truly present in the Lord's Supper, touching His divine nature, but that in the Lord's Supper, those who are partaking are truly strengthened and nurtured by the human nature of Christ. How is this possible if the human nature is not omnipresent? Calvin said He is made present to us by the divine nature.

In the New Testament, Jesus talks about going away and remaining, "Little children, yet a little while I am with you. You will seek me, and just as I said to the Jews, so now I also say to you, 'Where I am going you cannot come.'" (John 13:33). The disciples watched Him ascend into heaven, and yet He said to His disciples, "Even though I'm going away in one sense, nevertheless in another sense, I am with you always, even to the end of the age." Jesus talked about a presence and an absence. In addition, when Paul speaks about Christ's earthly ministry, he says that he never knew Christ "*kata sarka*," that is, in the flesh. He never saw Him in His earthly incarnation; the Apostle did not know Him during His earthly ministry. The Bible speaks of Christ being at the right hand of God, and the idea is that He's not here in terms of His visible, physical presence.

The Heidelberg Catechism speaks about this when it says, "Touching Christ's human nature, He is no longer present with us." The church has always understood that the human nature ascended on high. "Touching His divine nature," says the catechism, "He is never absent from us." Even though Christ in His human nature ascended to heaven, His divine nature remains omnipresent, and is particularly present in the church. Does that mean that at the time of the ascension, the human nature went to heaven and left the divine nature and that the perfect union of the two was disrupted? No. The incarnation is still a reality. It was a reality even at the death of Christ. At the death of Christ, the divine nature was now united with a human corpse; the human soul went to heaven and the human soul that was in heaven was united with the divine nature. The human body that was in the tomb was still united with the divine nature. So if we can understand that the human nature is localized because it is still human, the human nature is somewhere other than this world. However, the human nature, in heaven, remains perfectly united to the divine nature.

Remember that when you are in communion with the divine nature, you are in communion with the person of the Son of God and all that He is. When I meet Him here in the divine nature and enter into communion with the person of Jesus, this divine nature remains connected and united to the human nature. By communing with the divine nature, I'm not communing with just the divine nature; I'm also communing with the human nature, which is in perfect unity with the divine nature without having the human nature take upon itself the divine ability to be in all these different places. Remember, at no time is the human nature separated from the divine nature; thus, you can maintain the unity of the two natures and maintain the localization of the human nature without deifying the human nature. And yet, the person of Christ can be present in more than one place at more than one time by virtue of the omnipresence of the divine nature.

It is important to see the difference between this view and the Roman Catholic view. The Roman Catholic view empowers the human nature to come down to earth in all these different places at once. In this way, you can find the human body of Christ in as many Roman Catholic parishes as there are in the world. We're rejecting this idea because Christ's body is in heaven. We meet the actual person in all of our various churches and enter into blessed communion with the whole Christ by virtue of the contact we have with the divine nature, but His human body remains localized in heaven. This is consistent with the way Jesus speaks in the New Testament when He says, "I'm going away, yet I will be with you." The presence He promises of Himself in the New Testament is a real presence and real communion with His people.

Consider the Westminster Confession again:

> In the sacrament we partake not only outwardly the visible elements, but also inwardly by faith, really and indeed, but not carnally or corporally, but spiritually, receive and feed upon Christ crucified, all the benefits of His death: the body and blood of Christ being then not corporally or carnally in, under, or with the bread and wine; but really, as spiritually, present to the faith of believers, as the elements themselves are to the outward senses.

Because of the omnipresence of the Son of God in His deity, we really meet the whole Christ in the Lord's Supper and are nurtured by the Bread of Heaven.

One final note with respect to the Roman Catholic Church's teaching on the Lord's Supper. They believe that the Mass represents a repetition of the sacrificial death of Christ every single time it is celebrated. Christ is, as it were, crucified anew. Of course, the Roman Catholic Church teaches that there's a difference between the original sacrifice that Jesus made at Calvary and the way the sacrifice is rendered in the Mass. The difference is this: At Calvary, the sacrificial death of Jesus was one that involved real blood. It was a bloody sacrifice. The sacrifice that is made today is a sacrifice without blood. Nevertheless, it is a true and real sacrifice. It was that aspect, as well as the doctrine of transubstantiation, that caused so much of the controversy in the sixteenth century because it seemed to the Reformers that the idea of a repetition of any kind does violence to the biblical concept that Christ was offered once and for all. So in the Roman Catholic view of the sacrificial nature of the Mass, the Reformers saw a repudiation of the once–for–all character of the sacrificial offering that was made by Christ in His atonement (John 19:28–30; Heb. 10:1–18).

Chapter Seven

Blessing and Judgment

In addition to the doctrine of transubstantiation and the reenactment of the sacrifice of Jesus, there were other aspects of the Roman Catholic view of the Lord's Supper that were problematic for the Reformers.

Consider 1 Corinthians 10:14–22:

> Therefore, my beloved, flee from idolatry. I speak as to sensible people; judge for yourselves what I say. The cup of blessing that we bless, is it not

a participation in the blood of Christ? The bread that we break, is it not a participation in the body of Christ? Because there is one bread, we who are many are one body, for we all partake of the one bread. Consider the people of Israel: are not those who eat the sacrifices participants in the altar? What do I imply then? That food offered to idols is anything, or that an idol is anything? No, I imply that what pagans sacrifice they offer to demons and not to God. I do not want you to be participants with demons. You cannot drink the cup of the Lord and the cup of demons. You cannot partake of the table of the Lord and the table of demons. Shall we provoke the Lord to jealousy? Are we stronger than he? (1 Cor. 10:14–22)

Here Paul gives some strong warnings concerning the mixing of the Lord's Supper with idolatrous practices. Apparently, some of the Christians of Corinth participated in the Christian services as well as pagan feasts and festivals. This provoked Paul to address questions about eating meat that was offered to idols. Oftentimes after these pagan services were over, the meat they used for sacrifice was sold in the marketplace. Some Christians had scruples about this, saying, "I'm not going to have anything to do with any meat that participated in any way in a pagan ceremony." They believed that it was sinful to eat meat that had been offered to idols. Paul answered by saying that there's nothing inherently sinful about the meat. How it was used before it went on sale in the marketplace shouldn't cause any great concern for the Christians (1 Cor. 8).

From very early on, the church has had to struggle with the intrusion of idolatry into the practice of the liturgy, particularly with respect to the Lord's Supper. Returning to the question of transubstantiation, we remember that the problem that Calvin saw involved the deification of the human nature of Christ. Calvin said that this would be the most subtle form of idolatry possible. Because Christ is the God-man, He is the Son of God, and the New Testament calls us to worship Him. We worship the person, but we do not extrapolate the human nature from the divine and worship the human nature apart from its union with the Second Person of the Trinity. To worship the human nature of Jesus apart from its union with the divine Son of God would be to commit idolatry because it would be to ascribe to the created aspect of Jesus a divine element.

But we need to be very careful here. The church does worship the whole person of Christ, but He is worthy of worship because of His divine nature, not because of His human nature. So the Reformers, particularly Calvin, were concerned about practices in the medieval church relative to the worship of the human nature of Jesus.

If you walk into a Roman Catholic Church today you will notice that they genuflect. They bow one knee and then sit down. If you watch during the process of the Mass, the priest frequently genuflects in the middle of his activity as well. Why the genuflection? The object of the genuflection is the tabernacle. The tabernacle is usually a golden box that is prominently featured at the top of the altar, and in that golden tabernacle is contained the bread that has been consecrated. Roman Catholics believe that bread becomes the actual body of Christ. So the reason for the bowing and the genuflecting is to genuflect towards the consecrated host. Roman Catholics view that consecrated bread as an object of worship, and the Reformers greatly objected to this. They'd say, "Why would people be bowing before consecrated bread? Even if it became the human nature of Jesus, it would not be appropriate to be bowing down before human nature."

There was also another point that was a matter of controversy in the Lord's Supper. This had to do with the church's understanding of what actually happens in the drama of the Mass. After the consecration takes place, the Roman Catholic Church teaches that what happens in the Mass is the repetition of the sacrifice of Christ upon the cross. Now, the church makes it clear that this repetition of the sacrifice is done in a non-bloody way; nevertheless, they insist that the sacrifice is a real sacrifice. So even though it's a non-bloody offering, Christ is truly and really sacrificed afresh every time the Mass is offered. The Reformers found that to be blasphemous, as it was a complete rejection of what the book of Hebrews tells us, namely, that Christ offered Himself once and for all (Heb. 10:10). The sufficiency and the perfection of the atonement that Christ made on Calvary was so thorough that to repeat it would be to denigrate the supreme value of the once-for-all atonement that had been made there.

In the Westminster Confession of Faith 29.4, there is this statement:

Private masses or receiving the sacrament by a priest or any other alone, as likewise the denial of the cup to the people, worshiping the elements, the lifting them up or carrying them about for adoration, and the reserving them for any pretended religious use are all contrary to the nature of this sacrament and to the institution of Christ.

We see again that the Protestants reacted very strongly to the theology of the Mass, following Paul's warnings in 1 Corinthians 10. But 1 Corinthians 10 is not the only place where Paul gives warnings. He gives even stronger warnings in 1 Corinthians 11 with respect to the abuse of the Lord's Supper. Paul writes:

But in the following instructions I do not commend you, because when you come together it is not for the better but for the worse. For, in the first place, when you come together as a church, I hear that there are divisions among you. And I believe it in part, for there must be factions among you in order that those who are genuine among you may be recognized. When you come together, it is not the Lord's supper that you eat. For in eating, each one goes ahead with his own meal. One goes hungry, another gets drunk. What! Do you not have houses to eat and drink in? Or do you despise the church of God and humiliate those who have nothing? What shall I say to you? Shall I commend you in this? No, I will not. For I received from the Lord what I also delivered to you, that the Lord Jesus on the night when he was betrayed took bread, and when he had given thanks, he broke it, and said, "This is my body which is for you. Do this in remembrance of me." In the same way also he took the cup, after supper, saying, "This cup is the new covenant in my blood. Do this, as often as you drink it, in remembrance of me." For as often as you eat this bread and drink the cup, you proclaim the Lord's death until he comes.

Whoever, therefore, eats the bread or drinks the cup of the Lord in an unworthy manner will be guilty concerning the body and blood of the Lord. Let a person examine himself, then, and so eat of the bread and drink of the cup. For anyone who eats and drinks without discerning the body eats and drinks judgment on himself. That is why many of you are weak and ill, and some have died. But if we judged ourselves truly, we would not be judged. But when we are judged by the Lord, we are disciplined so that we may not be condemned along with the world.

So then, my brothers, when you come together to eat, wait for one another—if anyone is hungry, let him eat at home—so that when you come together it will not be for judgment. About the other things I will give directions when I come. (vv. 17–34)

It's obvious what's going on here. The memorial agape feast, which was celebrated in conjunction with the Lord's Supper in the early church and that which was to show forth Christ's death and the repetition of the Passover, became an occasion for unbridled gluttony and selfishness in the Corinthian community. People were pushing each other out of the way to get to the table to gorge themselves with food while others were left hungry. In other words, the whole point of celebrating the Lord's Supper was being destroyed by this behavior. So, Paul had to speak about two problems in Corinth. On the one hand, the mixing of idolatry with the celebration of the Lord's Supper and the denigration of the sanctity of the event by people who were turning it into a church picnic for gluttony. It's in this context that Paul gives these very sober warnings about the celebration of the Lord's Supper.

Because of this teaching, one of the strong principles that came out of the Protestant Reformation in reference to the Lord's Supper is what we refer to as "the fencing of the table." In some churches, before the celebration of the Lord's Supper, the minister will warn people who are not members in good standing of an evangelical church that they should not participate in the sacrament. He will remind the congregation that the Lord's Supper is only for Christian people who are truly penitent. There are even some churches that won't allow you to participate in the Lord's Supper unless you are a member of that particular congregation. If you're a visitor you're discouraged from participating even if you are a Christian.

The purpose of fencing the table is not to exclude people out of some principle of arrogance but rather to protect people from the dreadful consequences that are spelled out here by the Apostle Paul, where in this chapter he speaks of the *manducatio indignorum*, which means "eating and drinking unworthily." When a person participates in the Lord's Supper in an unworthy manner, instead of drinking a cup of blessing, they are drink a cup of cursing. They are eating and drinking unto damnation, and God will not be mocked. If people celebrate this most sacred of activities in the church and they do it in an inappropriate way, they expose themselves to the judgment of God.

Oscar Cullman, the Swiss theologian, said that the most neglected verse in the whole New Testament is 1 Corinthians 11:30: "That is why many of you are weak and ill, and some have died." Some scholars believe that the meaning of 1 John 5:16–17 is that God will not send Christians to hell who misused and abused the Lord's Supper, but He might take their lives.

The point that Paul makes here is that the sacrament of the Lord's Supper is a sacrament that involves and requires a certain discernment. We are to discern what we are doing. We are to come with a proper attitude of humility and repentance. Of course, the point is not to exclude people from the table. Nobody is worthy, in the ultimate sense, to come and commune with Christ. We, who are unworthy in and of ourselves, come to commune with Christ because of our need. But we are to come in a spirit of dependence, not arrogantly, confessing our sins and trusting in Him alone for salvation. If we handle these sacred things in a hypocritical manner God will not hold us guiltless. That's why we need to explore the significance of this sacrament.

In participating in the Lord's Supper, we meet with the living Christ, receive the benefits of communing with the Bread of Heaven, and yet at the same time we must keep ourselves from any form of behavior or distortion of this sacrament that would cause the displeasure of God to fall upon us.

About the Author

Dr. R.C. Sproul was founder of Ligonier Ministries, founding pastor of Saint Andrew's Chapel in Sanford, Fla., first president of Reformation Bible College, and executive editor of *Tabletalk* magazine. His radio program, *Renewing Your Mind,* is still broadcast daily on hundreds of radio stations around the world and can also be heard online. He was author of more than one hundred books, including *The Holiness of God, Chosen by God,* and *Everyone's a Theologian.* He was recognized throughout the world for his articulate defense of the inerrancy of Scripture and the need for God's people to stand with conviction upon His Word.

Free eBooks *by* R.C. Sproul

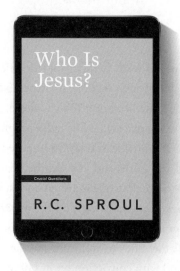

Does prayer really change things? Can I be sure I'm saved? Dr. R.C. Sproul answers these important questions, along with more than twenty-five others, in his Crucial Questions series. Designed for the Christian or thoughtful inquirer, these booklets can be used for personal study, small groups, and conversations with family and friends. Browse the collection and download your free digital ebooks today.

ReformationTrust.com/freeCQ

Get 3 free months of *Tabletalk*

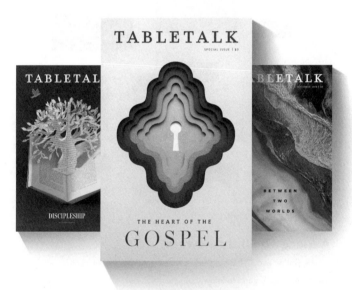

In 1977, R.C. Sproul started *Tabletalk* magazine.
Today it has become the most widely read subscriber-based monthly
devotional magazine in the world. **Try it free for 3 months.**

TryTabletalk.com/CQ | 800.435.4343

ASK LIGONIER

Do we have free will?

Why did God kill Uzzah?

Is it true that God controls everything?

A Place to Find Answers

Maybe you're leading a Bible study tomorrow. Maybe you're just beginning to dig deeper. It's good to know that you can always ask Ligonier. For more than forty-five years, Christians have been looking to Ligonier Ministries, the teaching fellowship of R.C. Sproul, for clear and helpful answers to biblical and theological questions. Now you can ask those questions as they arise, confident that our team will work quickly to provide clear, concise, and trustworthy answers. When you have questions, just ask Ligonier.

Supper is a foretaste of heaven. One day we will see the Bridegroom in all of His glory, and we will see the church offered to Him in its perfection. That's the future orientation of the Lord's Supper.